Middle-East   Asia   America

			c36 000 Primitive people in Lower Yellow River Valley	30 000 B.C. people hunted.			c25 000 – 17 000 B.C. Hunting people inhabit Canada, Mexico, Andes		c50 000 – 20 000 B.C. First migrants from Asia reached North America
Phoenicians	**Sumerians**	**Hebrews**	**Chinese**	**Japanese**	**Indians**	**Mayas**	**Aztecs**	**Incas**	**First Americans**

Timeline scale (B.C. above 0, A.D. below):
8000 – 7500 – 7000 – 6500 – 6000 – 5500 – 5000 – 4500 – 4000 – 3500 – 3000 – 2500 – 2000 – 1500 – 1000 – 500 – 0 (B.C./A.D.) – 500 – 1000 – 1500 – 2000

Date	Phoenicians	Sumerians	Hebrews	Chinese	Japanese	Indians	Mayas	Aztecs	Incas	First Americans
~4500			First pottery							
~3200		Oldest inscribed tablet at Kish								
~3000	Phoenicians settle									
~2500		Ur supreme				Civilisation in the Indus valley				
~2100			Semi-nomadic	Hsia Dynasty						
~2000	Egyptian, Babylonian, Hittite influence	Hammurabi of Babylon rules	Abraham, Isaac and Jacob							Pottery in southeast of North America
~1700			Egypt dominates	Shang Dynasty		Aryans invade				
~1500	Phoenicians trading in Mediterranean	First Assyrian Empire								Eskimo culture begins to use sea as a source of food
~1100			King David Israel & Judah	Chou Period				Culture in Mexico		
~1000	Carthage established							Climax of Oltec culture		'Mound Builders' inhabit Ohio Valley
~700	Persians dominate	Wars between Persians and Greeks	Assyrians Babylonians Greeks	Civil wars		Greeks reach India		First pryamids in Mexico		
~400	Greeks take Tyre		Romans take Judea	Ch'in Dynasty Han Dynasty	Yao period begins	Greeks expelled				
~200	Punic Wars									
~0	Roman domination		Hebrew lands fall to Romans; Hebrews without homeland until 1948, when Jews given Israel	chaos and unrest		Invasions				
~300 A.D.						Gupta Empire				
~500				China united	Classic Buddhist Japan	First Muslims rule				
~900				Sung Dynasty	Capital moved to Heian (Kyoto)		Maya civilisation in Yucatan	Aztec settlement on Lake islands	Machu Picchu built / Inca civilisation flourishes	
~1250				Yuan Dynasty Ming Dynasty	Civil war	Moghul Empire				
~1492				**Columbus reached the New World**						
~1500				Ch'ing Dynasty Opium Wars	Early Modern Japan			Spanish under Cortes capture Aztec lands	Spanish invasions of Inca and Maya lands	White settlers cultivate Virginia / African Negroes sold as slaves

The Chinese

The Chinese

Pamela Odijk

M

The Chinese

Contents

The Chinese: timeline

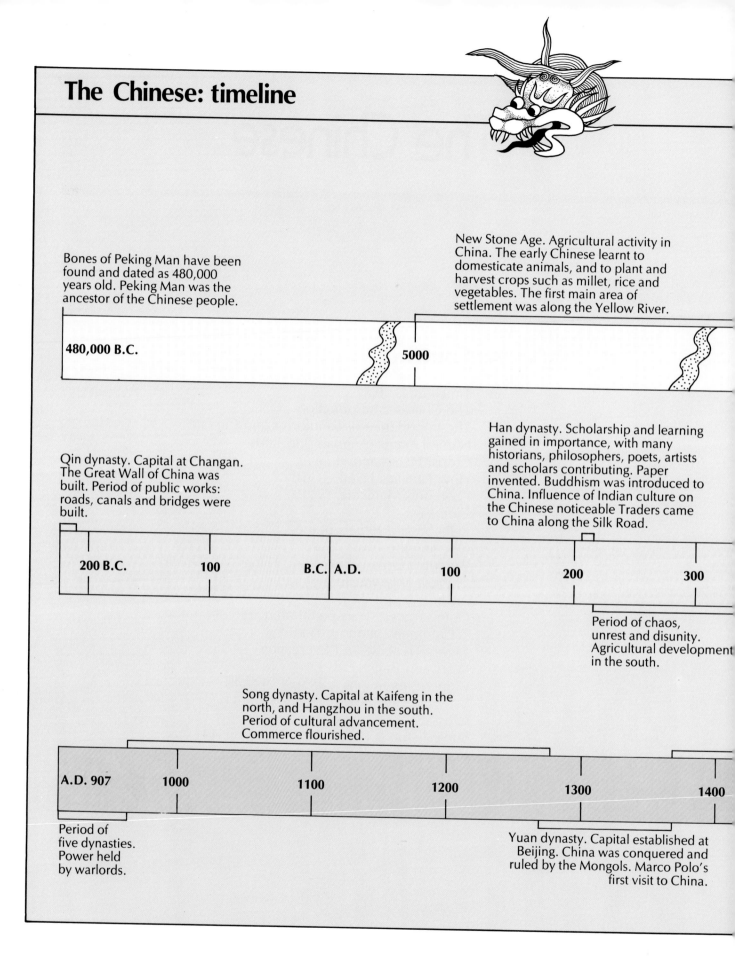

Bones of Peking Man have been found and dated as 480,000 years old. Peking Man was the ancestor of the Chinese people.

New Stone Age. Agricultural activity in China. The early Chinese learnt to domesticate animals, and to plant and harvest crops such as millet, rice and vegetables. The first main area of settlement was along the Yellow River.

480,000 B.C.

5000

Qin dynasty. Capital at Changan. The Great Wall of China was built. Period of public works: roads, canals and bridges were built.

Han dynasty. Scholarship and learning gained in importance, with many historians, philosophers, poets, artists and scholars contributing. Paper invented. Buddhism was introduced to China. Influence of Indian culture on the Chinese noticeable Traders came to China along the Silk Road.

200 B.C.   **100**   **B.C.** **A.D.**   **100**   **200**   **300**

Period of chaos, unrest and disunity. Agricultural development in the south.

Song dynasty. Capital at Kaifeng in the north, and Hangzhou in the south. Period of cultural advancement. Commerce flourished.

A.D. 907   **1000**   **1100**   **1200**   **1300**   **1400**

Period of five dynasties. Power held by warlords.

Yuan dynasty. Capital established at Beijing. China was conquered and ruled by the Mongols. Marco Polo's first visit to China.

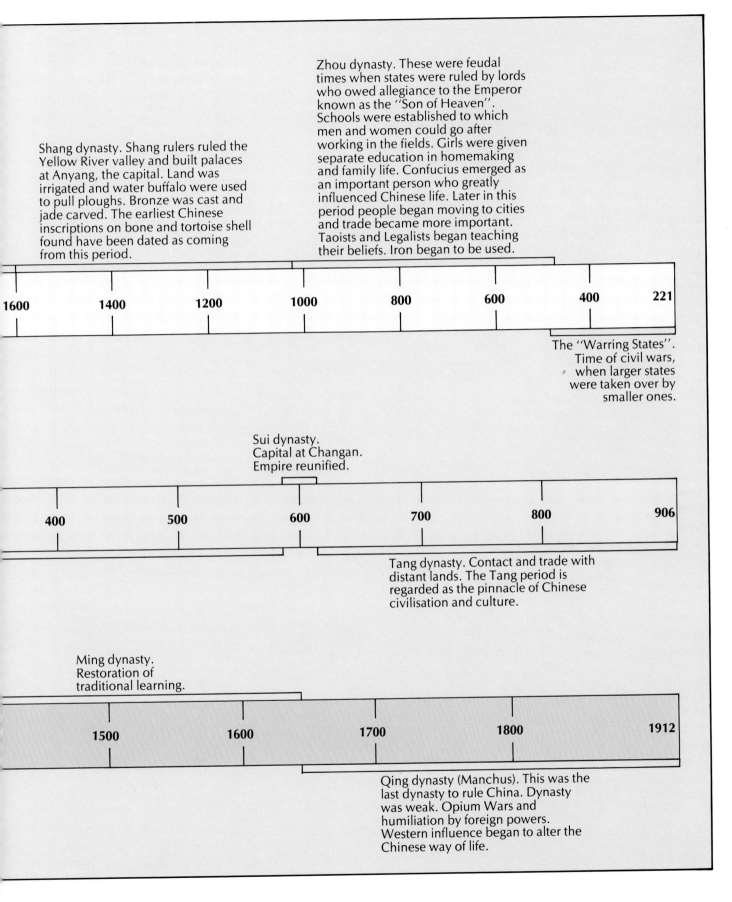

Shang dynasty. Shang rulers ruled the Yellow River valley and built palaces at Anyang, the capital. Land was irrigated and water buffalo were used to pull ploughs. Bronze was cast and jade carved. The earliest Chinese inscriptions on bone and tortoise shell found have been dated as coming from this period.

Zhou dynasty. These were feudal times when states were ruled by lords who owed allegiance to the Emperor known as the "Son of Heaven". Schools were established to which men and women could go after working in the fields. Girls were given separate education in homemaking and family life. Confucius emerged as an important person who greatly influenced Chinese life. Later in this period people began moving to cities and trade became more important. Taoists and Legalists began teaching their beliefs. Iron began to be used.

1600   1400   1200   1000   800   600   400   221

The "Warring States". Time of civil wars, when larger states were taken over by smaller ones.

Sui dynasty. Capital at Changan. Empire reunified.

400   500   600   700   800   906

Tang dynasty. Contact and trade with distant lands. The Tang period is regarded as the pinnacle of Chinese civilisation and culture.

Ming dynasty. Restoration of traditional learning.

1500   1600   1700   1800   1912

Qing dynasty (Manchus). This was the last dynasty to rule China. Dynasty was weak. Opium Wars and humiliation by foreign powers. Western influence began to alter the Chinese way of life.

7

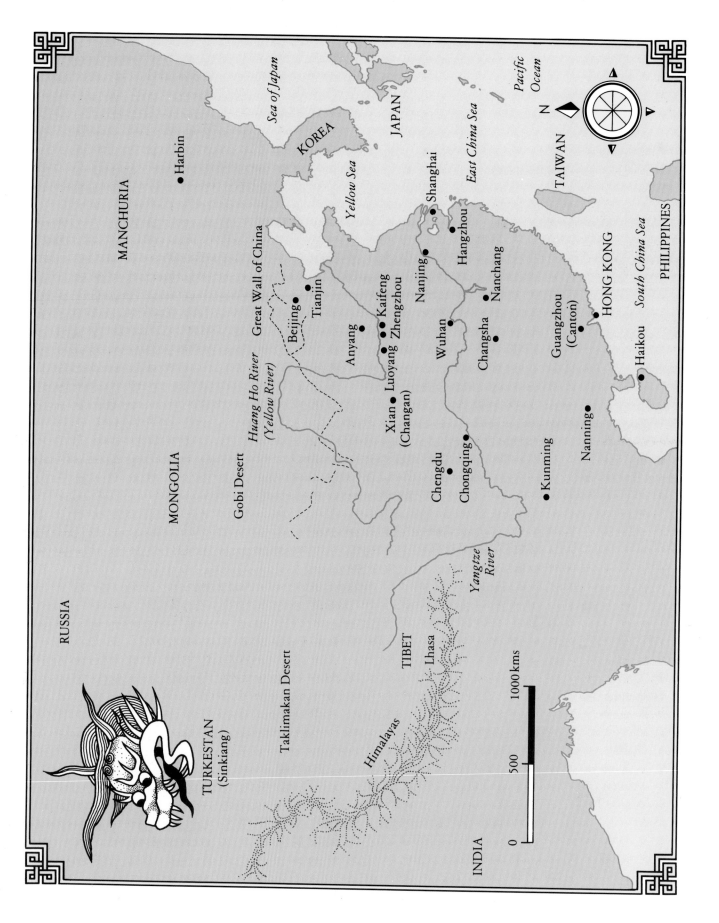

RUSSIA

MANCHURIA

Harbin

MONGOLIA

Sea of Japan

KOREA

JAPAN

Pacific Ocean

Gobi Desert

Great Wall of China

Yellow Sea

Shanghai

East China Sea

TAIWAN

N

Huang Ho River
(Yellow River)

Beijing

Tianjin

Kaifeng

Anyang

Luoyang Zhengzhou

Nanjing

Hangzhou

Nanchang

HONG KONG

South China Sea

PHILIPPINES

TURKESTAN
(Sinkiang)

Xian
(Changan)

Wuhan

Changsha

Guangzhou
(Canton)

Haikou

Taklimakan Desert

Chengdu

Chongqing

Kunming

Nanning

TIBET

Lhasa

Yangtze
River

Himalayas

1000 kms

500

0

INDIA

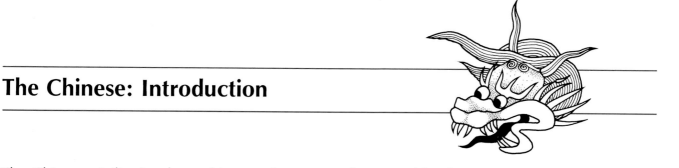

The Chinese: Introduction

The Chinese civilisation has a history of over 5,000 years and for most of this time the Chinese people saw no need to distinguish their country from any other. They sometimes referred to their country as "Under Heaven" or "The Middle Kingdom". They spoke of themselves as "Men of Han" after the famous Han dynasty, and "Men of Tang" after another dynasty. The advanced Chinese culture was discovered by the West during the time of the Romans. The Europeans began to be more interested in China after Marco Polo wrote of his travels there in the 13th century A.D. The Europeans called the country China, taking the name from the Qin **dynasty** at the start of the Chinese Empire.

The 4,000 years of Chinese civilisation has seen many changes and achievements yet there has always been a continuity. Each dynasty (or ruling family) made changes, and the history of the Chinese can be divided into the times of each dynasty.

The Great Wall of China was built during the Qin dynasty to protect the northern frontier.

Name of Dynasty	Some Important Things That Happened
Shang Dynasty 1600–1027 B.C.	Shang rulers ruled the Yellow River valley and built palaces at Anyang, the capital. Land was irrigated and water buffalo were used to pull ploughs. Bronze was cast and jade carved. Silkmaking was already known. The potter's wheel was in use.
Zhou Period 1027–475 B.C.	These were feudal times when states were ruled by lords who owed allegiance to the emperor known as the "Son of Heaven". Schools were established to which men and women could go after working in the fields. Confucius emerged as an important person. Later in this period people began moving to cities and trade became more important. Taoists and Legalists began teaching their beliefs. Iron began to be used.
The "Warring States" 481–221 B.C.	Time of civil wars.
Qin Dynasty 221–207 B.C.	Most scholars regard Qin as the beginning of the Chinese Empire. A common written language appeared. Strong government and a strong army were established. Roads, canals and bridges were built. The Great Wall of China was built. The capital was established at Changan.
Han Dynasty 206 B.C.–A.D. 220	Scholarship and learning gained in importance with many historians, philosophers, poets, artists and scholars contributing. Paper was invented. Buddhism was introduced to China. The end of this dynasty was marked by a period of invasions, war and unrest.
A.D. 220–589 Sui Dynasty A.D. 589–618	Period of chaos and unrest. Country united again.
Tang Dynasty A.D. 618–906	One of China's greatest dynasties when the military had much power and the economy prospered. Literature and education flourished. Buddhism introduced from India became part of the Chinese way of life. Block printing was invented.
Period of the Five Dynasties 907–960	Power held by warlords.
Song Dynasty 960–1279	Great cultural advancement especially in landscape painting. Moveable type invented.
Yuan Dynasty (Mongols) 1271–1368	The Mongols were the fierce warriors who conquered China but were bad administrators. Marco Polo's visit to China. Capital at Beijing.
Ming Dynasty 1368–1644	Famous for its ceramics, architecture and painting. The novel became increasingly important and was written in everyday language.
Qing Dynasty (Manchus) 1644–1911	This was a weak ministry. During the later part of the Manchu period Western influences began to alter the Chinese way of life.

The Importance of Landforms and Climate

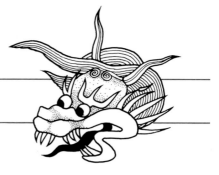

China is the third largest country in the world with the Pacific Ocean as its eastern boundary, tropical rainforests in the south, two great deserts in the north and north-west, and in the south-west rise the peaks of the highest mountains in the world, the Himalayas. Two large river systems run through China: the Huang Ho (Yellow River) in the north and the Yangtze in the south. Over the centuries the great rivers of China have flooded often causing destruction. However, the floodwaters carried with them silt from the uplands and deposited it on the lowlands and deltas. This silt kept the peasants' farms fertile, enabling them to continue to produce crops.

The vastness of the Chinese landscape experiences a range of climatic conditions. Ice covers much of the north during the winter months, while the southern ports in the summer are lashed with tropical monsoons.

The Lijiang River in south-eastern China. These hills were formed by erosion.

Climate

Northern China receives little rainfall as the southern mountain range prevents the monsoon rains from reaching there. Summers are hot and winters are cold. This part of China has always been referred to as the "brown north" because of the dry summers which cause the dry yellowish brown soils.

South China receives a high rainfall and has a subtropical climate with humid summers and mild winters. This is the "green south" where many trees grow. Streams and canals provide sufficient water for irrigation. Crops can be grown here all year round.

By being hemmed in by the largest ocean, the highest mountains and one of the biggest deserts in the world, ancient China was quite isolated from other peoples and cultures, although the Mongols did invade China from across the desert and established the Yuan dynasty (1271–1368).

Natural Plants, Animals and Birds

Plants

China has abundant plant growth which includes about 30,000 species, many of which are unique to China. Vegetation cover includes mangrove swamps, tropical rainforests, desert vegetation, savanna grasslands and temperate forests. Both evergreen and deciduous trees grow in China. Bamboo, which can be found in all parts of China, had many uses for the ancient Chinese as a source of food and as a raw material for building, furniture and tools.

China's plant resources range from region to region. Generally, in the northern areas chestnuts, limes, mulberry, millet, wheat, licorice, barley, hemp and pears grow. Jujube trees are also found in the north. In the southern and south-eastern areas rice, tea, camphor, cinnamon, bamboo, hemp and orchids grow. Sugarcane, ginger, citrus and fruits are found in both eastern and western areas.

In all, China has some 35,000 species of plants. Among the most unusual and ancient plants native to China are the Ginko or maidenhair tree and the dawn redwood tree. These species are so old they are referred to as living fossils.

Animals and Birds

An enormous variety of animal and bird life has always been found in China. Animals include pandas, lynx, leopards, wolves, tigers, bears, martens, badgers, ermine, weasels, foxes, raccoons, and mongeese. Hooved animals include many types of deer, antelope, gazelle, ibex, sheep, goats, yak, wild boar, ox, and various species of horse and wild camel. Until recent times the rhinoceros was found in the south-west. Elephants, now found in the south-eastern tropical forests, were once also found in the north.

China has about one eighth of the world's bird species which include hawks, pheasants, parrots, peacocks and kingfishers. The "gallus" or wild chicken, native to China, is the species from which domesticated chickens descended.

Fish have also been plentiful with over 1,000 species available. Among the reptiles are many turtles including the large freshwater turtle. The most primitive of all amphibians, the giant salamander which measures over 1.5 metres (5 feet) long, is also native to China.

Because China has had such an abundant plant and animal life since prehistoric times it has always been able to support a large population.

Bamboo forests can be found throughout China, and are home to the giant panda bears.

Above: the ibex is one of the many hooved animals that inhabit the desert and mountainous regions of China.

Right: the red panda, which lives in temperate bamboo forest areas of south-west China, is an endangered species.

Crops, Herds and Hunting

Throughout China's history, most people were engaged in agricultural activity. **Millet** was grown from the 5th millennium B.C., and rice from the 4th millennium B.C. The growing of wheat dates from about 1300 B.C. Most agricultural activity took place in central and western China. Today, this area is thought to have been the earliest and largest centre of agricultural activity in the world.

The Chinese ploughed their fields with wooden ploughs. The first iron ploughs came into use in 418 B.C. Water buffaloes were first used to draw ploughs in the 1st century B.C. In later times, other agricultural implements were invented and included a **three-share plough**, an implement that ploughed and sowed, and a **harrow**.

The planting and harvesting of crops was done by hand. A sickle or bill hook was used to harvest crops. Sheaves of harvested crops were carried from the fields suspended from the ends of long poles which were placed across the shoulders. Grain was threshed by beating it against a frame or flattening it on the ground. It was winnowed by tossing it in the air so that the wind could blow away the chaff letting the grain fall to the ground. Rice was husked by being pounded in a **mortar** by hand or by using a hand-turned mill.

In about A.D. 1100 water driven machinery was used to pump water onto rice **paddy fields** to irrigate them, and to drain fields when required, and to drive threshing machines. Around the fields were canals, ditches and dykes to hold and direct the water for rice growing. Ash and manure were added to the soil as fertiliser, and rotation of crops was practised to help keep the fields fertile.

Rice paddy fields in south-east China. The Chinese have cultivated rice for the last 6000 years.

Crops grown included peas, alfalfa, beans of many kinds including the soy bean, water chestnuts, and various other types of vegetables. Fruits included oranges, bananas, lichees, cherries, grapes, plums and nuts. The Chinese also grew raw materials for making clothes, including silkworms and their necessary mulberry trees, cotton, and plants which produce **hemp** and jute.

The Chinese kept various kinds of domesticated animals. Donkeys and mules were used more in the north, while in the south water buffaloes were more commonly kept. In the north, roads were wide enough to enable horse-drawn waggons and carts to be used to carry things, while in the south there were only narrow tracks between the rice fields. Along these tracks **farmers** would carry the loads slung across their shoulders on poles. In some places donkeys were used to carry loads.

Hunting and Fishing

Large quantities of fish were caught by the Chinese. Fishermen used a variety of methods including rodfishing and netfishing. From as early as 100 B.C. carp were being raised as a source of food.

Peasants kept pigs, chickens, and other birds as a source of food. Sometimes sheep, goats and cattle were kept, too. Hunting was considered a sport by the nobility, an activity they carried out in their personal game parks. Peasants could kill animals that threatened their crop fields.

Hunting was considered a sport by the nobility, as shown in this 17th century hunting scene.

How Families Lived

Houses

Houses of the wealthy and peasants were of similar design but varied in size, furnishings, decorations and the area of surrounding land given over to gardens and courtyards. They were built originally of rammed earth but later brick was used with either thatched roofs or tiles. The houses of the wealthy had many rooms grouped around a courtyard where rock gardens, shrubs, vines and bamboo were grown around pools which sometimes contained goldfish. All doors and windows which opened onto the courtyard were shaded with blinds (called *liene-tse*) made from damask, silk or woven bamboo. Wall hangings of birds, flowers and landscapes adorned the walls of the wealthy while poorer people had plain whitewashed walls or covered them with wallpaper.

Furniture was made from wood which was carved and then stained and lacquered. A bed was a prized possession and was usually made of lacquered wood and surrounded with embroidered curtains. In poorer homes, the bed was often a platform of bricks covered with a cotton-filled mattress.

In poorer homes heating and cooking was provided by a small coal burning **brazier**. Instead of wasting fuel heating an entire house, the Chinese preferred to put on heavier or extra layers of clothing.

Cities and Towns

Cities and towns were crowded places. Usually great wealth could be found beside great poverty. The narrow streets were market places where people met to buy and sell, and entertain and beg.

This traditional Chinese town house was built during the 16th century.

Harvesting the fields: both men and women worked in the fields.

Families

The family was the most important unit of Chinese society. Members of a family were expected to be loyal to one another and care for each other. The elder members of the family were the most respected. Especially the aged. The entire family was responsible for the behaviour of its members: honour or dishonour could be brought upon a family by the behaviour of its members. The family was regarded as being so important that when writing the three characters which made up a Chinese name, the character which designated the family was written first, the second was often identical for everyone of a particular generation while the last character was particular to the individual.

Men

Men were expected to marry by the age of thirty. The father was regarded as head of the house and a son was always considered a minor for as long as his father was alive. The head of the house was responsible for the conduct of everyone including the servants. Marriages were usually arranged. Though a man could only have one wife, he could purchase **concubines**. After marriage the bride lived with her husband or near his father's house where she served him and his mother for the rest of her life. A dowry was paid by the groom to the bride and thereafter his wife was regarded as the husband's property. The bride was also expected to bring a dowry of goods to her husband.

Most men were peasant farmers who tended their fields. Some were craftsmen in the provincial towns or the capital.

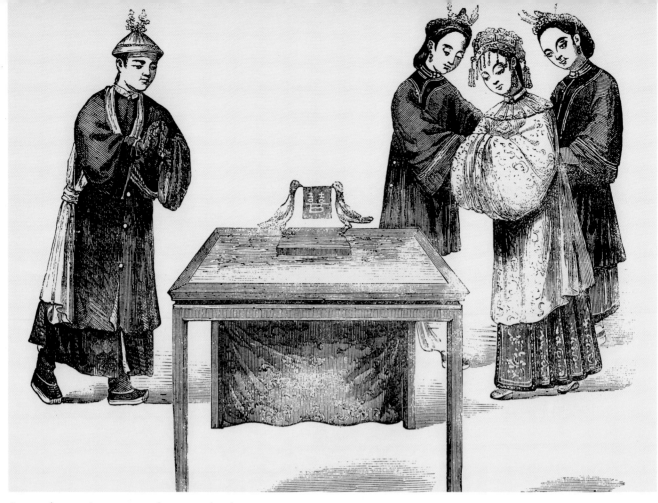

Form of a marriage treaty, drawn up by the parents of the bride and groom, to arrange the marriage and set the dowry.

Women

Women were expected to marry by the age of twenty. Chinese women had few rights. Their marriages were arranged and they were not even permitted to make their own will. Widows could have another husband sought for them, without their permission, by her parents-in-law. An abandoned wife could seek another husband with permission from the **Mandarins**. Women who left their husbands to remarry were severely punished.

Concubines had to obey and wait upon the legitimate wife. Concubine's children regarded the legitimate wife as their mother, and upon her death the children of the household were required to mourn for three years.

Women were responsible for the management of their homes. The management of silkworms and the production of silk was also women's work.

Children

Children were expected to implicitly obey their parents and were punished if they did not. If their father died, the respect was transferred to the eldest son. Boys were separated from their sisters at the age of seven, and from then onwards were never permitted to remain seated in their presence. Boys entered school at the age of ten, and at the age of fifteen they began to learn the skills of warfare. Girls were taught homemaking skills. They were taught to be modest and to obey their elders. Formal education was denied women.

As peasant families were very poor, money for even elementary education was not available. For those who could afford it, education was an important part of their lives. Boys learned from books made from bamboo and were required to learn by repeating and memorising. Education was to develop a sense of duty to others and to the state.

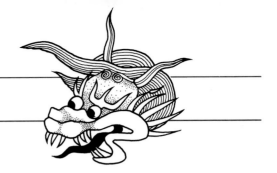

Food and Medicine

The great difference between rich and poor in China was evident at mealtimes. Poor people cooked their food and heated their rice wine on a small coal burning stove which also supplied heat during the cold months. Although rice was the main food and eaten by everyone, poorer people could only afford to eat meat twice a month or on special feast days. In the northern provinces, wheat was grown as well as rice for food. Wheat flour was used to make noodles and small cakes which were steamed.

Wealthier Chinese ate poultry, fish, water fowl, pork and venison, and the very wealthy demanded sharks' fins, bear paws, and the feet, tails and tongues of other rare animals. Large quantities of vegetables were eaten by everyone and included beans, turnips, melons and yams. Meals were spiced with relishes, pickles and sauces.

Food was served in small dishes from which people selected their individual helpings. Food was eaten from small bowls with **chopsticks**.

Most Chinese ate twice a day, at mid-morning and at dusk. A typical meal for a peasant in the fields would have been a bowl of rice, some green vegetables, bean curd and perhaps a fish cooked in oil, and tea. Tea was introduced to the Chinese from the southern lands after the Han dynasty and rapidly became popular. There were special utensils for brewing and drinking it. Wine was made from grapes as well as from fermented grains. Herbs, flavourings, sugar and fruits were added to vary the flavour. Salt was a precious commodity in areas far from the sea but from the 2nd century B.C. it was extracted from underground deposits using drills.

A Chinese bowl decorated with coloured glazes made in the 11th century A.D. during the Sung dynasty.

Feasts

Rich men's banquets were elaborate and could include up to forty courses. These banquets had strict rules of etiquette. An invitation to such a meal would be given three times in writing: the first on the day before, the second on the morning of the day and the third when the banquet was ready.

Guests were served first with wine which was drunk in a ritual manner: the cup was lifted to the forehead, then below the table level, and then the entire contents would be drunk. Many varieties of food would be continuously served. Tea would be served before the sweets were prepared. During this time the guests would retire to the garden while the actors and entertainers were served. The guests would then return for the remainder of their meal. These banquets usually lasted for at least six hours. Each guest was expected to write a letter thanking the host for his hospitality the next day.

Medicine

The Chinese studied and practiced medicine from very early times. They believed in the presence of **Yin** (female elements) and **Yang** (male elements) in the human body in association with other things. The presence and proportions of Yin and Yang were thought to determine many things including health, and Chinese medicine attempted to control this. This was done in many ways.

Herbal remedies relied upon included the most expensive herb **ginseng**. **Acupuncture** and **moxibustion** were also used extensively. Acupuncture was a treatment which involved pricking the body of the patient with needles at specific places to effect a cure. Moxibustion involved burning a specially prepared herb on the skin. Special attention was given to vitamin

Above: 16th century ivory statue of the mythical physician Pien Ch'iao and the magician Chang Shen Kung.

Below: acupuncture chart showing the points where the needles are inserted, (Ming dynasty 1368–1644).

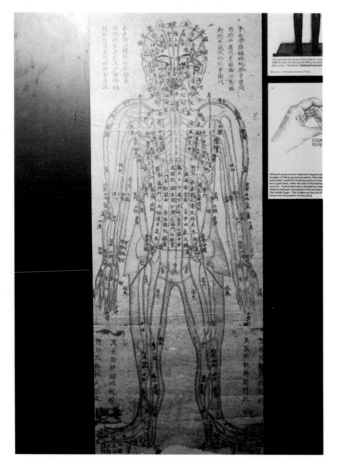

deficiency diseases including beriberi, and minerals such as iron and copper were also used in remedies.

Chinese medical treatise are the oldest in the world. Medical encyclopaedias were compiled under the Tangs and medical books were written during the Song dynasty. A medical college was established under the Song dynasty but most medical students studied an apprenticeship with a practicing physician. Buddhist temples also served as hospitals.

The Chinese were also superstitious people and believed that some illnesses were brought about by evil spirits, especially in ancient China. For those illnesses, a special doctor called the *tao-tze* was called who went about the house making loud noises to drive the evil spirits away.

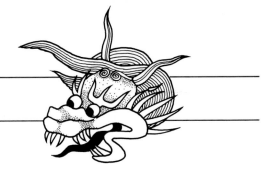

Clothes

Many different styles of clothing have been worn by the Chinese throughout their history. Perhaps the most popular was the kimino style garment which the Japanese adopted and adapted.

Most clothing was made from cotton. In the lower Yangtze Valley, cotton was a major crop. Peasants' work clothes were made from a coarse fabric that was woven using the fibres of a plant called **ramie**.

Emperors, nobles and rich people wore garments made from silk. Silk was the most famous cloth of ancient China. Silk was made from the cocoons of the silkworm.

Imperial Dress

Men and women of imperial and noble rank wore *chi-fu* or "dragon robes" which were long and elaborately patterned. They had long tubular shaped sleeves. The skirt of the *chi-fu* did not quite reach the ground which enabled the wearer to walk easily. Colour indicated rank and status. The emperor's chi-fu was always yellow and decorated with the twelve imperial symbols.

The *p'u-fu*, or three-quarter length purple coat was worn over all special occasion garments. This too had a special brightly coloured insignia to indicate the rank of the wearer.

Men's Headdress

Chinese men wore their heads shaved except for a long plait called a *pene-se*. Most men wore a small funnel shaped cap with a red silk tuft. Mandarins and scholars wore a similar shaped cap made of satin (red inside, and white outside) and adorned with various kinds of ornaments which indicated their status. Important men and scholars wore their finger-nails excessively long in early times to show that they did not engage in manual labour.

Women

Modesty dictated that women only show their faces. As such their long tunics were buttoned at the neck, and reached down to their feet.

The Phoenix robe, which belonged to the empress dowager Tzu Hsi, the last empress of the Qing dynasty (1644–1911).

Over their tunics they wore long robes with enormous sleeves which covered their hands. On their feet they wore embroidered satin slippers.

Wealthy women spent many hours bathing in ornamental baths using fragrant oils, and dressing in fine clothes of silk and cotton.

Peasant women in the country wore trousers like the men but in the towns they covered their trousers with skirts.

Women wore their long, straight black hair wound into large rolls and pinned high on their heads with flowers and ornaments. Upper class women used cosmetics such as rouge on their lips and cheeks, rice powder as a facial powder and blue, black and green grease paint on their eyebrows. These cosmetics were kept in a small mirrored box.

Above: early in the 20th century foot binding was outlawed. Still, some elderly women bear the results of this traditional practice.

Below: portrait of an ancestor (17th century painting on silk).

Bound Feet

Foot binding was introducing during the Song dynasty (960−1279). Female children who were born into wealthy families had their feet bound at an early age. Though small feet were considered a sign of beauty, it meant that even as adults, walking short distances involved great difficulty. This ensured that women did not venture far from their homes.

Peasant women who were required to help in the fields did not practise foot binding.

Colours

Colours for clothes were regulated. Special white clothes were worn when mourning the deceased. Children were not allowed to wear white clothes while their parents were still alive. Yellow was only worn by the emperor and princes. Mandarins were allowed to wear black, blue and violet. On feast days they could wear satin garments which had a red background. Black and blue were the colours worn by ordinary people.

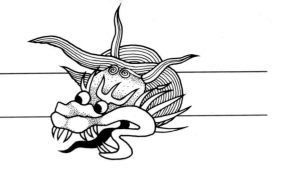

Religion and Rituals of the Chinese

China has been called the land of three religions: Confucianism, Taoism and Buddhism. Confucianism and Taoism were purely Chinese teachings, while Buddhism came to China from India during the Han dynasty in the 1st century A.D. The three religions complemented each other, giving the individual a place in society (Confucianism), a place on earth (Taoism) and a hope in a future life, (Buddhism).

The Chinese believed in a creator god who could view the past, present and future. They also believed in ancestor spirits. Sacrifices were offered in the open to the creator god, and to the ancestor spirits. Later, temples were constructed for this purpose.

Confucianism

Known in China as Kung Fu-tse, "the holy master" or "wisest sage", Confucius (551–479 B.C.) was a learned scholar who became a Mandarin. After the death of his mother he went into mourning for years, during which time he contemplated the meaning of life. He spent the rest of his life travelling, teaching and writing to guide people, and he became very influential. His main aim was to establish a stable society founded upon virtue, goodness and morality.

Followers of Confucius believed in the importance of the family, respect for the aged and their wisdom, and a commitment to social order. Confucius wanted people to act harmoniously without the need for written laws.

The Dafu, a 71 metre (233 feet) high Buddha carved into a cliff overlooking the junction of three rivers in Sichuan. This is the largest Buddha in the world. The ears are 7 metres (23 feet) long. The project was begun in A.D. 713 by a monk who hoped that the presence of Buddha would subdue the swift currents of the rivers and protect boatmen.

Buddhism

Buddhism was introduced into China by Indian merchants. Buddhist teachings were based on those of Siddharta Gautama (later called Buddha) who was born in Nepal in about 560 B.C. Buddha taught that people should live without great self-denial or indulgence, and that they should be moderate in all things. Buddhists believed in reincarnation, **karma**, and **nirvana**. Reincarnation is the belief that a person has more than one life. Karma is the belief that what you do in this life affects your

status in your next life, and also that your status in this life was determined by your conduct in your last life. Nirvana is the belief that a state of universal peace can be achieved.

Buddhist ceremonies were held at temples, and included praises, readings from sacred books, and the use of musical instruments such as bells, drums and cymbals. Offerings of rice and tea were also made. Many homes had Buddhist shrines, and pilgrimages were made to sacred places.

Taoism

Taoism was another important religion that developed in China. Taoism differed from Confucianism. It is thought to have been founded by a scholar named Laozi (Lao Tzu), and was based on a belief in nature rather than society. Tao meant "the way", and Taoists opposed any constraints placed on an individual which prevented that person living in harmony with nature.

The emblem of the Taoists was the Yin and Yang symbols: Yin, the passive female force, and Yang, the active male force.

Taoists believed there should be no conflict between these forces. Wayside altars to many Taoist gods were built throughout the country-side and paper money was often burnt at these altars as offerings to local spirits.

Reverence for Ancestors

Temples and ceremonies where ancestors could be honoured were present in China before the time of Confucius, as ancestor worship was a Chinese way and belief that eventually became a part of Confucianism. Some families had their own ancestral temples where ceremonies took place. Ceremonies included making offerings and incence burning.

17th century painting of Taoist sages admiring a painting of the Yin and Yang symbol.

Ceremonies and Rituals

Marriage

Marriages were arranged. A dowry would be paid and the families would sign an agreement concerning the marriage. A lucky day of good omens would be chosen as the wedding day and, until the wedding day, the groom and bride were forbidden to see each other although they were expected to exchange letters. The bride could receive gifts of rings, earrings and hairpins from the groom. For three days before the wedding no music was permitted in the groom's house and all lights remained on in the bride's house.

Superstition, Fêng Shui and Astrology

The Chinese were also very superstitious people who believed in lucky and unlucky days and places. Some people believed that evil spirits brought disease and illness, and wore charms to ward off the *kuei* or spirits. Fortune tellers assisted people in determining lucky and unlucky days for marriages, funerals and journeys. There was also a belief called *fêng shui* (wind and water) which was based on the belief that forces existed which operated for good or evil. Specialists in *fêng shui* would help individuals discover places with good influences or help people alter or avoid places or circumstances where evil influences were thought to exist. Astrologists were consulted in much the same way.

New Year

This was held on the fifteenth day of the first month of the New Year, and was the most elaborate Chinese festival. (The festival extended over several days from the thirteenth to the sixteenth day.) Lanterns of all shapes and sizes were a feature of the New Year and thousands of them were alight everywhere. Fireworks and feasting were also part of the celebrations.

Funerary figure of a warrior on horseback, from the Tang dynasty A.D. 618–907.

Death

The Chinese regarded the day of death as a day of honour for the deceased. A person would prepare for death well in advance by purchasing a fine coffin. If the family was poor, the eldest son might sell himself as a bonded servant to earn enough money to purchase a coffin. On the day of death, the deceased would be dressed in fine clothes, placed in the coffin, and friends and relatives would come to show their last respects by **kowtowing** before them. White, the colour of mourning, would be displayed.

Chinese funeral processions were more like parades. Men carrying paper statues would lead followed by others carrying burning perfumed oils. Musicians would follow, and then the coffin, covered in purple silk, carried by four bearers would come next.

Ceremonies conducted at the graveside included burning of paper houses, paper clothes and other symbols. It was believed that these items would be transferred to the spirit world of the departed.

Obeying the Law

The Chinese word for their kingdom was "Middle Kingdom". This expressed how they saw themselves positioned in the world, that is, at the centre of the universe. The Chinese regarded the world as a balanced whole. If a person or group upset this balance and harmony, they were to be punished. If whoever was responsible for upsetting the balance could not be found, someone was required to restore this balance. Chinese laws relied on collective responsibility rather than individual responsibility.

Influence of Confucianism, Taoism and Legalism

The aim of Confucian teachings was to persuade all people to take their proper place in life and to work for the benefit of all. Confucius believed that official positions should be given to people according to their talent, ability and education, not according to their birth and status. Confucius defined four types of people:

> the highest type of people were those who were born wise; next were those who became wise through learning; next came those who learnt by overcoming dullness; the lowest type of people were those who were dull, and who wouldn't learn.

As such, inferiors were to serve superiors, and superiors were responsible for the welfare of inferiors.

Taoists believed that society and the laws of society were the source of suffering. They believed that people should follow "the way" of nature, and live in harmony with nature. "The way" would lead people back to peace, contentment and a simple life.

The Legalist school of philosophy taught that people were basically evil and as such, conflict was inevitable. They believed in strict laws and in the emperor enforcing these laws, which were necessary for peace and security. The Legalists did not believe that moral guidance and philosophy were enough. These three groups had a strong influence on Chinese society and its laws.

The oldest complete Chinese law code that exists is the Tang code which dates from A.D. 653. Chinese law remained quite different from Western law until the 20th century when Western law was enforced in China.

Interior of the Palace of Heavenly Purity, which is inside the Forbidden City in Beijing. The emperor handled state affairs from the Palace of Heavenly Purity.

Writing it Down: Recording Things

The earliest Chinese inscriptions on bones and tortoise shell date back to 1500 B.C. during the Shang dynasty, and are records of **divinations**. These inscriptions were picture-writing questions to gods. Heat was applied to the inscribed shell or bone, and the resulting cracks were interpreted as answers. The Chinese had 3,400 characters of which about 2,000 are now understood. Writing on bone was followed by the use of bamboo strips, silk and then paper made from bark, especially the bark from mulberry trees.

In A.D. 105 Chinese paper was invented. This paper was made from various products such as tree bark (especially the mulberry tree bark), bamboo, hemp and rice straw. Chinese ink was usually black. Although red ink was made from sulphine of mercury its use was considered an imperial privilege.

Printing

The Chinese developed a printing process sometime between the 4th and 7th centuries A.D. Chinese printers carved their text on blocks of pear or jujube wood. The characters were carved so that they were raised on the blocks. They were carved in reverse. The carved characters were then painted with a strong paint. Sheets of paper were applied to the top of the blocks and gentle pressure was applied using dry brushes. Each sheet of paper was then peeled off the blocks and sewn together to make books. The earliest known printed book using this method was a Buddhist text, the *Diamond Sutra*.

Moveable Type

Moveable type was invented during the 11th century A.D. Each Chinese character was represented on a separate clay block, which could be singled out and glued to an iron block. After printing, the iron plate was heated and the single character blocks were loosened and removed. Because Chinese writing can involve the use of 1000s of characters, the setting of these iron plates could take quite a long time. Printing eventually reached Europe in the 15th century.

The Diamond Sutra, *printed in A.D. 868, is the world's earliest dated printed book.*

The Chinese Calendar

The Chinese became accurate astronomers as they developed their interest in the stars and planets. They recorded sun spots, **eclipses**, **supernovae** and comets. They calculated the length of equinoxes, solstices and months. Their observations (without the use of telescopes) led them to calculating the length of a year as 365¼ days, by the 14th century.

An **orrery** or mechanical model of the solar system was erected by the Chinese between A.D. 1088 and 1092. It was operated by a waterwheel and had a series of figures which indicated the time. This clock had no face or hands but struck the hour. This was a forerunner of the modern mechanical clock which was invented by the Chinese six centuries before mechanical clocks made an appearance in Europe.

Weights and Measures

Measures were based on parts of the body such as the distance from the pulse to the thumb. There was no unity in weights and measures until the 3rd century A.D. when Shi Huangdi the emperor of the Qin dynasty introduced a standard system. Some of these units were:

> *shih* or *tan* (basic unit) = 60 kilograms
> (132 pounds)
> *chich* and *chang* = 3 metres (9.8 feet)

Measures for grain not only depended on the capacity of the vessel used but also a full vessel had to produce a particular pitch when struck. This meant that vessels used for measuring had to be both a uniform shape and a fixed weight.

Numerals and Mathematics

Chinese numerals are older than the earliest number systems developed in Europe.

The Chinese relied on mechanical tools such as counting rods and the **abacus** to make calculations. (A Chinese abacus was called a *suan-pan* which meant computing tray). Their system allowed for the calculation of negative numbers by using different colours (black and red) from as early as the Han dynasty in 206 B.C. Because the Chinese used mechanical tools to make calculations there was no record of how a problem was solved or an answer reached. It was not until Western mathematics was introduced into China that the writing down of calculations became a part of mathematics.

Inscribed wooden strip from the Han dynasty. The poem reads:
The sun is hidden from view by dark clouds,
The moon is concealed by sand swept up by the
*   wind.*
I follow the waters of the Meng River, like the
*   Yellow River and the Yangtze.*
The waters flow and roll in waves.
I did not climb up when I reached Bi
For the gate of heaven is narrow so I walked
*   to the Peng pool,*
How could I climb up there without help? . . .
It is difficult to pass the gate.

Chinese Legends and Literature

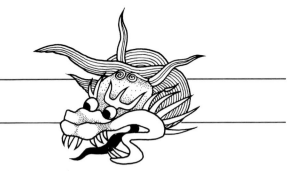

The earliest Chinese literature consisted of hymns and ceremonial songs sung at festivals. The first collection of Chinese poetry was called *Shih Ching* (*Classic of Poetry*). It contained some 305 songs and was written in about 500 B.C. during the time of Confucius.

There is a close connection between Chinese literature and Chinese music as most poetry and long ballads were originally written to be sung with musical accompaniment.

By the time of the Song dynasty there were books written in the old literary language and books written in everyday language. During the Yuan dynasty (1279–1368) a great number of plays were written.

The Chinese continued writing in their own traditions until the 19th century when there was increasing contact with Europeans. After this many Western works were translated into Chinese, and Chinese works were translated into other languages as well.

Myths

The ancient Chinese did not have a great many myths of their own, whereas in later times numerous mythological characters and gods were worshipped. Confucius and his followers had little use for myths and this affected the telling, collecting and believing of them, as Confucius was very influential in Chinese society. Han scholars worked out some of the ancient texts. By the end of the Zhou dynasty (475 B.C.) legends from India had become popular in China.

The Chinese myths are about gods and other supernatural creatures thought to affect people and the world. They were used to explain things that people could not otherwise understand.

Limestone relief depicting the pilgrimage of the boy Sudhana. Buddhist legends from India became popular in China.

Some Legendary Gods and Goddesses

Shang Ti (Lord on High) (who sometimes appears as *Ti chün*)	Controller of fate. Only the emperor was allowed to approach this god and offer sacrifices, and not people of lower rank.
Ch'ih Yu	Ch'in Yu sought the support of humans to overthrow Shang Ti. People who refused were killed. Others complained to Shang Ti who ordered Chung and Li to set up a barrier separating heaven and earth.

After this

Chung	became administrator of heaven, and
Li	became administrator of earth.

However, heaven and earth were kept apart by a platform supported by four pillars. *Kung Kung*, a heavenly god fell against one of these pillars thus causing the heavens to slant.

Nü Kua	A goddess of marriage who refashioned the pillars by using turtle feet. In some legends she fashioned people from mud. In other legends she was the bride to Fu Hsi, China's first legendary emperor.
Chu Ying (Chu Lung)	A god with a human face and the body of a red snake. He opens his eyes, day arrives and it becomes night when he closes them.
Hsi	Son of Li, who helped administer the sun and moon. He had a human face and legs growing out of his head. (He had no body or arms.)
Hsi Ho	A wife of Ti Chün who created ten suns. One sun would be sent out on duty each day while the other nine would sit on the giant fu-sang tree on the eastern edge of the world. (The jo tree was at the western edge.) In some legends the sun travels in a chariot pulled by a dragon and Hsi Ho is the charioteer.
Ch'ang O (Ch'ang Hsi, Heng O)	A moon goddess, also wife of Ti Chün, who created twelve moons. In another legend she is wife of Hou I who fled to the moon and was changed into a toad.
She Chi	Spirits of soil and grain.
Hou T'u	Spirits of humanity and deceased emperors.
Hou I	One day all ten suns appeared in the sky making a heatwave. Hou I shot nine suns from the sky with white arrows fired from a red bow, so they drowned in the sea and the earth was saved. In another legend he also saved the earth from six monsters.
Yü	Tamer of the Flood who, assisted by dragons and tortoises, dredged outlets to the sea for the rivers. Yü made the earth suitable for humans to live on and grow crops. There are many stories about him and the water animals.

Legendary Heroes, Heroines and Emperors

Fu Hsi	A god with a serpent's body who knew the secrets of divination and writing. He taught people many skills including hunting and cooking. (Nü Kua was his wife.)
Shen Nung	Succeeded Fu Hsi. Invented the cart and plough and taught people how to use fire, tame oxen, yoke horses, as well as other agricultural skills. He collected 365 plants useful to medicine.
Huang Ti (Yellow Emperor)	Born on the Earth (Yellow) Day. He introduced mathematics and the calendar, and invented building bricks and the compass. Built the first altar and made the first sacrifice. Brought the first bamboo to China and made the first musical instruments.
Ts'an Nü (Lady of the Silkworm)	Huang Ti's wife. Taught women how to breed silkworms and how to make silk.
Lord K'ai	He wore two black snakes in his ears, rode two dragons and visited heaven three times. Brought to earth the first songs.
K'uei	He made the first music by beating his belly with his tail.

The Dragon, the Phoenix and the Unicorn

The dragon (*lung*) features in many Chinese myths. Dragons bestow blessings and benefits but occasionally can be wicked. They have the power to become invisible. Chinese dragons are never slain in stories about them.

The phoenix (*feng-huang*), the female counterpart of the dragon was not known in ancient China but appears in later myths. The phoenix is usually associated with music. Phoenix ornaments are often worn at weddings.

The unicorn (*ch'i-lin*), was the minder of spring and protector of saints and sages.

19th century ivory figure of Shen Nung, the Chinese medical god.

Art and Architecture

Painting and Calligraphy

Calligraphy, the art of writing, was considered the supreme art and greatly influenced Chinese painting which was also done using a soft brush with bristles set into a wooden handle. Muscular control had to be practised to perfect light and delicate strokes in both arts.

Artists tried to express the forces of the universe through their painting.

Chinese painting achieved its greatest height during the 10th to 14th centuries. Unfortunately many Chinese paintings have been lost, mainly because materials used were perishable and were destroyed in wars and fires. Silk was the most common material upon which artists painted but paper was also used.

Jade

This was called yü by the Chinese and came from various kinds of rock. It was especially prized. It was believed to be indestructable and was used for making ceremonial objects, objects to be placed in tombs to protect the dead, jewellery, vases, belts, screens, bowls and ornamental flowers.

Below: bronze tripod vessel made during the Shang dynasty, 12–10th centuries B.C.

Above: Chinese pottery jar, 11–12th centuries A.D.

Pottery and Porcelain

Although Chinese potters were slow to become masters of their craft, they eventually led the world in the design and manufacture of beautiful pieces. Porcelain was China's most distinctive art and it replaced stone art. In the time of the Ming dynasty (1368 to 1644) fine white porcelain (commonly called china) was being made. By the time of the Qin dynasty (1644) Chinese porcelain had become popular in Europe and colours used included pale green, and shades of blue and purple.

Bronze

Magnificent bronze vessels from the Shang dynasty have been found. These were used in religious sacrifices to the ancestors. Bronze vessels were cast in sectional moulds.

The Forbidden City in Beijing was built in the early 15th century.

Lacquerwork

Lacquerwork began as an art in China and later spread to Japan. Because lacquerwork objects were perishable not many have survived.

Lacquer was obtained from the sap of a particular tree, processed and mixed with colouring substances. It was then applied to an object with a brush. Lacquer was used to cover and decorate wood, metals, porcelain and cloth. Some items were also inlaid or painted with silver and gold. Lacquer soaked cloths were placed over moulds and images to make masks.

Textiles

Silk was not only used to make clothes but also to make decorative silk panels, scrolls, covers and tapestries. The earliest surviving examples date from the Tang dynasty (A.D. 618 to 906) and had simple patterns of flowers, ducks and lions. Later tapestries were woven with gold and silver threads, with the finest tapestries being produced at the time of the Manchus (A.D. 1644 to 1912).

Architecture

Throughout their history the Chinese have erected buildings with gigantic walls but because they used inferior materials, very little architecture from ancient times has survived. All Chinese buildings had the common characteristics of order and symmetry, and many were designed and built in such a way so as to ensure safety should an earthquake occur, as they frequently did in China.

The roofs of Chinese buildings were unique and a very prominent part of the design. Some buildings had double and triple roofs, each one rising above the other and being supported by pillars. Often coloured glazed tiles such as the yellow roof tiles of imperial palaces and the blue tiles of the Temple of Heaven were used. The upturned curved eaves and gable ends were also favoured by Chinese architects and builders. Some of the most beautiful Chinese architecture is in the Forbidden City in Beijing.

Courtyards were another feature common to houses, temples and palaces. As the Chinese rarely built buildings of more than two storeys, they extended the area with courtyards which were landscaped with gardens.

Going Places: Transportation, Exploration and Communication

Trading interests took the Chinese to many places. Overseas trade in spices, dyes, perfumes, cotton fabrics, gold and precious stones was conducted from very early times both by sea and land.

By the time of the Ming dynasty in A.D. 1368, so much valuable cargo went to and from China that the trading ships became known as "treasure ships". As well, smaller ships took astronomers, cartographers and botanists to and from many places.

19th century painting of a Chinese junk. By the 9th century, Chinese junks were making safe voyages to India. By the 15th century, junks had become the largest, strongest and most seaworthy ships in the world.

Waterways

From earliest times the Chinese had shown great skill in using inland waterways. Almost every navigable stream and canal had its boat traffic, and locks were built to transfer boats from one level to another. Craft used on these ranged from ocean going **junks** to **sampans** and rafts. Barges were used along the smooth wide rivers to carry produce. In the upper areas of some rivers like the Huang Ho and the Yangtze, the rapids were dangerous and boats and barges were often carried overland on the return trip. Paddle-wheel ships were used on rivers in the time of the Song dynasty during the 10th and 11th centuries. Some were large enough to have several decks and up to eleven wheels on each side.

Roads

Even before the Zhou dynasty China had developed the oldest known network of roads for everyday use. It was important in a country as large as China that communication was as fast as possible. There were five grades of roads: pathways for men and pack animals, roadways for narrow-wheeled vehicles, roadways for larger vehicles, roadways where vehicles could pass each other, and roadways where three waggons could move abreast.

Roads were well-built and had stone surfaces. Travellers were able to cross rivers by ferries and bridges. Roads were often crooked, especially in the steep mountains, and steps and stairs were often cut into the sides. Courier stations were established along the roads so important messages could be sent quickly.

The famous Silk Road was the name given to the caravan route which led from China to the West through Sinkiang, Turkestan, Central Asia, Persia and Syria.

Music, Dancing and Recreation

Music and Dance

Chinese music has a long history and has always been regarded as an important part of ritual and education. Confucius and others were concerned with the moral influence of music, and Buddhism had its own special compositions. In Confucian temples there was banquet music (*yen yüeh*) and ritual music (*ya yüeh*). Common music was referred to as *su yüeh* and during the Tang dynasty (7th to 9th centuries A.D.) a new category was added, *hu yüeh* (foreign music), which became incorporated into Chinese culture. Also during the Han dynasty the *Yüen Fu* or the Music Bureau began to collect official and popular songs and musical scores.

Chinese musical instruments included chimes, bells, drums, bamboo pipes, lutes, clappers, gongs, cymbals, flutes, guitars and zithers.

Confucian rituals included military dances (*wu wu*) and civil dances (*wen wu*), both of which were accompanied by many musicians. Tiles in tombs from the Han dynasty show very informal and large dance groups, and paintings from the Tang dynasty show entertainers with many instruments and dancers.

Theatre: Drama

From the 13th century onwards drama was an important part of Chinese life. Performances were often given on outdoor stages which could be dismantled and moved elsewhere. Pantomimes which commemorated the deeds of ancestors were popular.

Temples were used for dramatic performances even when these had nothing to do with religion, and drama groups would often perform at markets and fairs. Very little scenery was used but elaborate costumes and masks were worn.

Other Recreations

Flying kites was enjoyed by both children and adults. Chess was always a popular game but was played slightly differently than in the West. The chess pieces were placed on the points of intersection of the squares and not on the squares. Other recreations included cock fights, horse and dog racing, playing ball, **shuttle-cock**, swimming, wrestling and fishing. Skating was a popular pastime during the cold winters. Gambling was favoured by the Chinese and included one particular game called *liu-po* which used sticks marked like dice. *Fantan* was also a gambling game played with coins covered with a bowl.

Opera singers performing a traditional Chinese opera in the Gardens of Performing Arts. In the foreground are the musicians. The performers' costumes are elaborate compared to the simple sets.

Folk Festivals

The best known folk festival was the Dragon Boat Festival which took place on the longest day of the year. Sacrifices were made to the river gods on this day.

Silk scroll from the 10th century A.D. depicting musicians at court.

Ching Ming was the chief spring festival when the dead were remembered. It was also a time of picnicing and feasting. Other festivals included the harvest festival, Confucius's birthday, and the festival of the coming of the first frosts in the north. Firework displays were a part of all Chinese festivals.

Wars and Battles

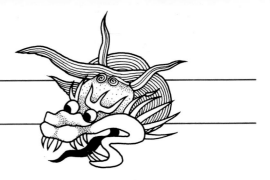

The early Chinese feudal armies were not powerful enough to be able to conquer other lands. The northern areas however were frequently invaded by people from Central Asia. The Great Wall of China was built as protection against the invading Mongols. The period 481 to 221 B.C. of Chinese history was known as the "Period of the Warring States", because armies of various **warlords** continually waged war against each other. Also in early times there were many battles fought on water.

During the Han dynasty, feudal armies gave way to professional armies as China grew politically powerful. It was during the Han period that China gained most of its present land area.

Arms and Armour

Soldiers went to battle on foot or in horse-drawn chariots protected by an armour of animal hide (buffalo or rhinoceros) and armed with bows and arrows tipped with bone or bronze. Some weapons of bronze were richly inlaid with silver and gold. The Chinese often adopted the motifs and clothing of the armies against whom they fought. They soon learned to adopt the wide trousers and boots of the central Asian armies and to go into battle on horseback as their enemies did. The Chinese also invented a better horse harness and a saddle which kept the rider in place. (Stirrups were not invented by the Chinese until the 2nd century B.C.) Horses were also bred in large numbers for the army.

Jade spearhead with bronze and turquoise from the Shang dynasty, 13th century B.C.

Military Examinations

For admission to official positions in the army, a series of military examinations had to be passed. Candidates were tested on military pursuits and were required to write essays on military subjects.

37

Better Weapons

The crossbow appeared in China in about 400 B.C. and two types were used: a small magazine crossbow and another larger mounted one which was effective against mounted cavalry in seige warfare. Later iron-plated armour, sometimes with fine chain mail, was used together with other protective clothing of padded quilted coats and, of course, helmets.

Gunpowder

Gundpowder had been invented in China in the 9th century A.D. and fire arrows were used in the 10th century. By the 11th century flame throwers and a kind of grenade projected by a catapult were used. The Chinese blunderbuss, a canon made of bronze, was in use by 1332.

The Opium War and After

From the 19th century, China found herself at war with Western powers who wanted to trade in opium and other products from India and the East. Fighting began when an English ship fired on a Chinese ship. This war has always been referred to as the Opium War although it was not just about opium. The Treaty of Nanking in 1842 opened many Chinese ports to the West.

Warrior from the tomb of the first emperor of the Qin dynasty. From these figures it is possible to know what battle clothes the warriors wore.

Chinese Inventions and Special Skills

Silk

The making of silk fabric from fibres made by the silkworm is thought to have begun in China as early as the 3rd millennium B.C. Silkworm farming was the work of women. Silkworms were raised on mulberry trees. The female moth laid her eggs on the leaves, and caterpillars (larvae) which hatched from the eggs fed on them. The caterpillars then spun a cocoon of silk around their bodies as they became pupae. The cocoons would be collected and boiled before the adult moth had a chance to emerge from the cocoon. (The moth would eat its way through the cocoon, cutting the silk thread, if it was allowed to emerge.)

Silk fabric became an item of trade during the Han dynasty (206 B.C. to A.D. 220). Silk was exported to Europe along the Silk Road. For many centuries only the Chinese knew how to control the life cycle of the silkworm, and how to wind the silk threads without damaging them. The weaving of silk on a drawloom was also Chinese knowledge. The Greeks took the knowledge of silk production to Persia and Italy.

Astronomy

The Chinese recorded all events they saw in the sky from very early times. They drew up charts and observed meteorites, eclipses, sun spots, supernovae, and comets. Halley's Comet was first observed in China in 240 B.C. The Chinese invented the armillary sphere at the time of the Han dynasty (206 B.C. to A.D. 220). This was an instrument of rings marked in gauges and hoops which divided the sky up so it could be mapped and measured. A smaller version called an orrery was built in the 1st century A.D., and was water-powered. The orrery imitated the movement of heavenly bodies.

Porcelain

Though the origins of porcelain production are unknown, it is generally thought that porcelain was first made in China during the Han dynasty (206 B.C. to A.D. 220). The glazing and painting were done by special craftsmen. The Chinese produced several grades of porcelain: the finest was for the emperor's use only; the second grade of porcelain was for the emperor to give as gifts; while third grade porcelain was for everyone's use. Chinese craftsmen produced a variety of porcelain pieces from grotesque figures, to figures so light that they could float on water.

Paper

Paper was discovered in China during the 1st century A.D. It was made from tree bark, hemp, old rags and fishing nets. Before the invention of paper the scribes carved their characters on bone and bamboo, and calligraphy was done on silk.

The Chinese kept the art of papermaking a secret for about 500 years. By the 8th century A.D., the Japanese had learnt of papermaking from the Chinese. Later traders and Chinese missionaries took paper to the West where it eventually replaced papyrus and parchment.

Printing

Printing was one of China's greatest achievements. It is thought to have been developed between the 4th and 7th centuries A.D. so that copies could be made of the writings of Confucius, the Buddhists and the Taoists. Chinese printers carved their text on blocks of pear or jujube wood, in relief. The carved blocks were then inked and stamped on sheets to make a

Casts of wooden type, A.D. 1300.

print. This method was used to print official histories.

Moveable type was invented during the 11th century. Each character was carved on a separated clay block. The characters could then be arranged and glued onto an iron block, inked and printed. Because written Chinese contains thousands of characters, the setting of blocks took a long time. Despite this, moveable type revolutionised the printing industry.

By the 15th century, printing had reached Europe.

Gunpowder

Gunpowder was discovered by the Chinese long before it was known of in Europe. At first, gunpowder was only used for fireworks during court and public festivities. It wasn't until the 11th century that the Chinese learnt how to use gunpowder in warfare.

There were different types of gunpowder: black gunpowder was used in explosive grenades and bombs which were hurled through the air at the enemy using catapults. Another type was used in signal rockets and flame throwers, and yet another type was used for large guns and cannons.

Cast Iron

Chinese metallurgists used an iron casting process similar to that used for bronze long before cast iron appeared in Europe. Reusable multi-part moulds enabled the Chinese to cast plough-shares and tools, and to produce them in great numbers. The use of iron tools enabled the land to be cleared more effectively, and canals and roads to be constructed more easily.

Medical Skills

Chinese medicine, which has a history of several thousand years, is based on the idea of equilibrium and dynamic balance between two opposing forces. Health is seen as harmony between the forces, and illness as imbalance. Chinese medicine used acupuncture, moxibustion and herbal remedies.

Compass

The Chinese were using the compass by the time of the Han dynasty (206 B.C. to A.D. 220). The compass was made using a piece of lodestone (magnetised iron ore) suspended on a piece of polished board. The lodestone rotated until it came to rest at a north-south position.

Later the lodestone was replaced by a flexible needle which was magnetised by rubbing it with a piece of lodestone. The compass was used mainly to work out sites for temples and buildings. The Chinese didn't use their compass as a navigational devise until the 11th century.

Other Chinese Inventions

The wheelbarrow was invented in China in the 3rd century B.C. The breast and collar harness was invented for draught animals so that they could pull heavier loads. The Chinese also invented bore-drilling as a means of obtaining water, suspension bridges made from bamboo, and lacquer, a natural varnish used to preserve and decorate many things including pottery and porcelain.

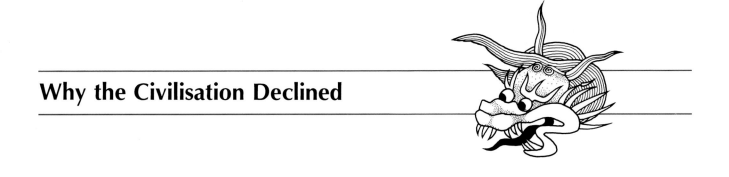

Why the Civilisation Declined

By the time of the Ming dynasty (1368 to 1644), China had the largest empire in the world and the Chinese had far reaching contact with other people. Their voyages had taken them far afield, and after the time of Marco Polo's land journey to China during the 13th century, the Europeans became very interested in faraway China.

As Europe became industrialised it became more powerful, and extended control over the Chinese. China after the Ming period was subjected to fierce attacks which could not be resisted.

Within China itself the position of the Emperor had been weakened either because the Emperor himself was a weak leader or because he died leaving an heir too young to rule in his own right and temporary rulers were not always strong. The people also had become dissatis-

fied with the way things were and a rebel leader Li Tzu-ch'eng emerged. His forces finally captured Beijing in 1644. He claimed the title of Emperor but sought the help of the foreign Manchus to retain power. However, on entering China, the Manchus claimed their leader as Emperor and the Manchu (Qin) dynasty remained in spite of its weak rulers until 1912 when the last of the Manchus were driven out.

During the reign of the Manchus, the empire was repeatedly attacked by the now industrialised and powerful Western nations who gained control of the important Chinese ports. This was made easier because China's defence had been allowed to become weak and inefficient under the Manchus.

After 1912 China entered a time of social and political upheaval and cultural change. The old ways were gradually changed and a new Chinese civilisation emerged which was much different from that of ancient and traditional China.

Young school children in China, today.

Glossary

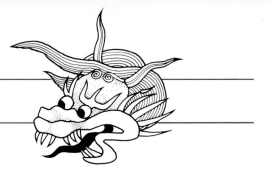

Abacus This was a mechanical tool consisting of beads strung on wires set in a frame used for counting and making calculations. It was called a *suan-pan* or "computing tray".

Acupuncture A process whereby a long, sharp metal needle is inserted into the underlying tissue of the skin at carefully chosen points to cure various ailments. The process dates back to 2500 B.C.

Astrology A study which believes that the movement of heavenly bodies has an influence on human affairs. Astrology required a great deal of recording of unusual occurrences in the heavens and masses of records of observations were collected and accumulated over time. The title *t'ai shih ling*, given to the imperial historian originally meant astrologer as well.

Astronomy A study of the heavenly bodies including their movements, positions, distances, magnitude and occurrences.

Billhook A cutting tool used for harvesting crops. It consisted of a blade with a hooked point which was fitted into a handle.

Bodhisattvas Buddhas who have renounced their right to nirvana and came back to earth to help others become enlightened.

Calligraphy The art of writing. The Chinese thought of calligraphy and painting as being closely related and both needed the expertise of using a brush pen. In China calligraphy is an honoured art form. Some important Chinese calligraphers were Wang Hsi-chich (321−379 A.D.), Su Shih (1036−1101 A.D.) and Mi Fei (1051−1107 A.D.).

Carp A large freshwater food fish which was bred in ponds and used for food.

Chopsticks A pair of thin sticks made of bamboo, wood or ivory, and used by the Chinese as eating utensils.

Comet A celestial body which moves about the sun in an elongated orbit. It has a central mass surrounded by a mist extending into a tail.

Concubine A secondary wife who lives in a man's house without being legally married to him.

Delta That part of the river near the sea where the river slows down and fans out over the plain. The river sediment is dropped in this area. The Huang Ho (Yellow River) has one of the most fertile delta regions.

Divination A practice which attempts to discover hidden truths or foretell the future by supernatural means such as reading the future in the lines of the *I-Ching*, or reading the design on the shell of a tortoise, or by the movements of the stars.

Drawloom A type of weaving loom used for weaving intricately figured fabrics. It was first used in the East for silk weaving and was later introduced to Italy during the Middle Ages.

Dynasty An hereditary ruling house or family. The founder of each dynasty was the first emperor of that dynasty and his successors ruled until the dynasty was eventually overthrown.

Eclipse An obscuring of light by another object. In a lunar eclipse the moon is partly or totally within the earth's shadow. In a solar eclipse the moon is between the sun and the earth.

Emperor The supreme ruler of the empire. The early emperors claimed to be "Sons of Heaven" and had the authority to govern all earth. The emperor was expected to oversee the administration of the country and to lead important ceremonies. Great respect was shown to the emperor and his family by all his subjects.

Ermine A small furred animal like a weasel which turns white in winter. The fur of the ermine was sought after and worn by people of rank or on ceremonial dress.

Ginseng A plant with an aromatic root which was used extensively in Chinese medicine.

Harrow An agricultural implement with teeth or discs which was drawn over ploughed land to level it and break up clods of earth.

Hemp A tall annual herb which was often cultivated. The tough fibre was used for making coarse fabrics and rope.

Herbal Remedies Medical cures and remedies which rely on the use of natural herbs. The Chinese used over 700 herbs in their medicines.

Jade Jade was especially prized by the Chinese who used it for making many objects. It was originally quarried in China but later also imported from Turkestan and Burma. It was believed that jade promoted immortality and would protect a body from decay.

Junk A classic Chinese sailing vessel with a high stern and projected bow and capable of carrying up to five masts. Each square sail was made of linen and slats of bamboo. They were highly efficient craft in which the Chinese made voyages to Indonesia and into Indian waters.

Karma A Buddhist belief. It means that a person's conduct in one life is rewarded or punished in future lives; and that one's position is this life was determined by one's conduct in the last life.

Kowtow A Chinese way of showing reverence and worship by kneeling before the person or object and touching one's forehead on the ground.

Mandarin A member of any of the nine ranks of public officials in the Chinese Empire. They were distinguished by a particular kind of button on their caps.

Mortar A bowl-shaped vessel of very hard material in which substances are pounded. Rice was pounded in a mortar.

Moxibustion A medical cure or technique supposed to remove pain by burning a special herb on the injured part of the body.

Nirvana A Buddhist belief. It means reaching a state of ultimate peace and happiness, and freedom from pain and worry and the present external world.

Orrery Apparatus for representing the motions and phases of the planets in the solar system.

Paddy Field A field which can be kept flooded so rice can be grown.

Pagoda A sacred tower of many storeys and upturned eaves. Coming originally from Buddhist ideas, the pagoda was developed by the Chinese and given a particular style. Pagodas were originally built in wood but later were also built of stone and brick.

Ramie An Asian shrub from which a fibre was obtained to make textiles.

Reincarnation A belief that the soul, upon death of the body, moves to another body or form.

Sable A small mammal resembling a weasel valued for its dark brown fur.

Sampan A common small Chinese boat of which there were many designs. Nearly all had large sterns and sharp bows and were usually rigged for sailing but could be rowed with oars.

Shuttlecock A piece of cork with feathers stuck in one end and batted to and fro with a bat or racquet in a game. (Used today as described here in the game badminton).

Sickle An implement with a long curved hooklike blade set in a short handle. It was used for harvesting grain.

Sun Spots Dark patches which appear regularly on the surface of the sun.

Supernovae Large brilliant stars which appear in the sky where no stars had been before. The Chinese kept records of these which have been of great interest to 20th century astronomers.

Three-share Plough A plough that cuts the ground in three places and raises it into mounds.

Warlords Powerful generals who ruled the provinces as separate countries. There were frequent wars and struggles between the warlords and their armies inflicted much suffering on the people.

The Chinese: Some Famous People and Places

Yun-kang and Lung-men Caves

These are Chinese Buddhist cave-temples created in the 5th century A.D. in the north of Shanxi Province. The caves contain fine examples of the first major influence of Buddhist art in China. There are about twenty major cave temples and many smaller ones. Some contain large statues of Buddha which were equated with the first five emperors of the Northern Wei (386–534). Other caves are more like worshipping areas. The first of these cave temples was constructed in about 460 at the instigation of a Buddhist monk named Tan-yo. When the Northern Wei court was moved to Lo-yuan in 494, new cave temples were constructed at Long-men.

The earlier artistic style in these temples was Indian in character but in later times a more Chinese style was acquired, this being particularly noticeable in the caves at Lung-men where images of Buddha show him clothed in the dress of a Chinese scholar.

The Long-men caves are located in the Honan Province. These were begun at the end of the Northern Wei dynasty and continued until the Tang dynasty. The most famous of these caves are the Ku-yang cave, the Pin-yang cave and the Feng-hsien Ssu which is an enormous cave which took three years to carve.

Marco Polo

Marco Polo was born in Venice in about A.D. 1254 and died in that same city in 1324. He was a merchant and adventurer who travelled across Asia to China. He spent 25 years in Asia, including 16 or 17 years in China as guest of the emperor Kublai Khan. His book *Il Milone*, known as the *Travels of Marco Polo*, describes people and things seen in his travels. It also contains fabrications and exaggerations.

The book was written while in a Genoa prison and with the help of a fellow prisoner Rustichello, a writer of romances and laws of chivalry. The book was an instant success in Europe where people had previously known little about Asia and China. An authentic copy of the book no longer exists. There are about 140 different manuscript versions of it in many languages and dialects.

The Empress Wu

Empress Wu, the female "Son of Heaven", was the only woman to occupy the position as Empress of China. She was born in A.D. 625 and became a concubine in the palace of the Tang emperor, Tai Tsung, at age thirteen.

Upon the death of the emperor, Empress Wu was sent to a Buddhist Convent but was brought back to the palace by the new emperor. She became Empress in 655 and exercised complete power when the emperor was ill during the last 23 years of his life. She eliminated her rivals and governed the empire efficiently. The Empress Wu selected the military leaders who conquered Korea.

From 690, at the age of 65, the Empress took the throne as Empress in her own right. She chose her administrators for their ability and loyalty and not for their social standing. She changed Chinese society from one controlled and governed by the military and aristocracy to one governed by a scholarly bureaucracy. In spite of her ability she was disliked by the conservative Chinese society whose power she had threatened and in some cases removed. She was also largely ignored by many Chinese historians who disliked her ruthlessness, cruelty and the fact that she did not conform to the traditional role of women in Chinese society.

She retired in 705, and her son succeeded her.

Laozi

Laozi is thought to have been the founder of Taoism and to whom the *Tao-te Ching*, an important Taoist writing, has been attributed. Very little is known about his life. It is thought he was born in the eastern part of what is now Honan Province and was an important official at the royal court of the Zhou dynasty. He is believed to have met Confucius, but many scholars dispute this. Scholars also doubt if the whole of the *Tao-te Ching* could have been the work of one person.

However, by the later Han dynasty, Laozi was a mythical figure who was worshipped by many people including the emperor. There are many legends about him and his birth, and some legends describe how Laozi adopted several personalities throughout his life, and after his death returned to earth several times to instruct Taoist teachers.

The Confucianists regarded him as a philosopher while the Taoists regarded him as a god.

Mencius

Mencius (Mengtzi) was an early Chinese philosopher who was born in about 371 B.C. He was considered to be a wise sage of Confucianism, second to Confucius himself. He was eventually called *ya sheng*, or "second sage". His father died when he was three and his mother took great care with his upbringing and education. (His mother has often been used as an example of a perfect Chinese mother.)

Mencius admired the talents of another pupil, Zezu, who was the grandson of Confucius and thereby gained his insight and commitment to Confucianism. He eventually became a teacher and travelled widely advising princes and administrators to govern humanely and to provide for the welfare of the people. However, most princes refused to adopt his principles.

The book *Mencius*, records his sayings and doings. Mencius believed and taught that when a ruler is no longer benevolent (*jen*) or righteous (*li*), his mandate of Heaven is automatically withdrawn and he should be removed from power.

Hsieh-Ho

Hsieh-Ho was a Chinese painter of the 5th century who invented the "Six Principles" of Chinese painting. These principles were creativity, disciplined brushwork, proper presentation of objects, specific colouring of those objects, good composition, and study by copying old masters.

Li Po and Tu Fu

Li Po was a Chinese poet who lived from A.D. 701 to 762 and rivalled Tu Fu (born 712 and died 770) for the title of China's greatest poet.

Li Po lived as a Taoist recluse at the age of 19 but was later married and lived with his wife's family. He was later accepted into a group of poets who wrote verses for court functions. Although Li Po became famous he disliked this situation and took once more to a nomadic life. During his wanderings he met another poet, the then unknown Tu Fu.

Li Po eventually became a poet to the Prince Lin in 756 but was later thrown into prison when the Prince was accused of attempting to set up an independent kingdom. Li Po was eventually released, then re-imprisoned and banished. He finally died in eastern China.

Tu Fu was educated in Confucian tradition but failed his Imperial Examination in 736 so did not qualify for a government position. He spent his youth travelling and writing poetry. He learned about Taoism while travelling with Li Po but he later returned to his original religion. He admired Li Po's work but after their initial travels they did not meet again.

Tu Fu eventually gained a court position through his poetry which often contained political messages. He married in 752 and settled down to life on a farm. He was involved in the An Lu-shan Rebellion which brought down the Tang dynasty. His life was one of hardship and several of his children died of starvation. He died in 770.

His poetry criticised war, the luxury and extravagance of the imperial court, and showed his compassion for people. He was master of all poetry forms including the *lu shih* of "regulated verse".

Index

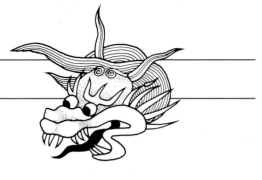

46

Acknowledgements

The author and publishers are grateful to the following for permission to reproduce copyright photographs and prints:

Australasian Nature Transparencies: (Tony Howard) cover, (Frithfoto) p.9, (Otto Rogge) pp.11, 12, 35, (Silvestris) p.12, (Frédy Mercay) p.13 top, (Pavel German) p.13 bottom, (S. Hodgkiss) pp.22 top right, 23, 26, (Peter McDonald) p.41; Coo-ee Historical Picture Library pp.17, 18; Ronald Sheridan/The Ancient Art and Architecture Collection pp. 15, 19, 20, 24, 25, 27, 28, 29, 31, 32, 34, 37, 38, 41; Werner Forman Archive pp.21, 22 left bottom, 33, 36.

Cover design and maps: Stephen Pascoe

First published in Australia by
THE MACMILLAN COMPANY OF AUSTRALIA PTY LTD
107 Moray Street, South Melbourne 3205
6 Clarke Street, Crows Nest 2065

Published simultaneously in Great Britain in 1989
by Macmillan Publishers Limited,
4 Little Essex Street, London, WC2R 3LF.

Associated companies and representatives
throughout the world

British Library Cataloguing in Publication Data

Odijk, Pamela
    The Chinese.
    1. Chinese civilisation, to 960
    I. Title II. Series
    951'.01

    ISBN 0-333-52085-8

Set in Optima by Setrite Typesetters, Hong Kong
Printed in Hong Kong